Microfinance in Africa

The paradigm Shifts

Teresa Maru-Munlo

Contents

ACKNOWLEDGEMENTS

I'm grateful to a few colleagues and friends who happily shared their experiences, corroborating or validating my own experiences. Many thanks to Chris Kizza, Fletcher Chilumpha and Victoria Kalua. I'm also grateful to my long-time colleagues Beatrice Odiyo, Mathew Macharia, Moses Banda and many others who have shared part of my journey with added humour.

I'm grateful to various institutions and many individuals who believed in me and gave me opportunities to experience microfinance first hand. While I cannot mention all of them because the list is so long, I would like to single out Abla Benhammouche and say many thanks for her support and faith in my work.

My warmest gratitude is reserved for my daughters, Paula Munlo and Paullete Munlo, who have been my number one cheerleaders. These young girls urged me to share my experiences and encouraged me to go on with the understanding that writing is not a race.

Teresa Maru-Munlo

March 2023

CHAPTER 1

IN MY BEGINNING, THERE WAS MICROFINANCE

For over thirty years, I have worked in the microfinance sector in various capacities and in several African countries, mostly East and Southern Africa. This started in the late eighties in Kenya when the approach to microfinance was more integrated with client training as a prerequisite to credit followed by constant monitoring and follow up after loan disbursement. At the time, traditional donor funding flowed like a never-ending river. For any microfinance institution, even reaching 1000 clients was a significant achievement. Field monitoring was done in branded motor vehicles courtesy of generous donations and grants. This issue of branded vehicles tickles me to date. I remember attending an interview with an organisation that required its field staff to use motorbikes. They asked me, during the interview, if I could use a motorbike, to which I responded in the negative. So, continuing with the interview, they asked if I would be willing to learn to ride a motorbike and move from the city to some remote town. Being a youngster and inexperienced, I responded that it would be a demotion to move from using a car to a motorbike, worse still, to move from the city to some remote town I had never heard of. As you might guess, I failed the interview in the first round, not because of my technical expertise but my attitude! My friends passed the interview and went on to earn twice as much as I was earning, and that really pained me. But a few months later, I got myself a better job with a special focus on training small business owners, and I did that job for one and a half years before I found myself back in microfinance.

When we were employed, we were oriented to serving the poor, and I remember visiting clients in a slum area as part of my orientation. Having come from a not-so-affluent background, I fitted in easily as my personal aspirations matched those of the financial service providers; my heart and head were definitely in the right place. Looking back, I remember colleagues with similar aspirations, and we all banded together regardless of the institutions we worked for, and some of us have remained in touch with each other thirty years later. Two organisations stand out in my memory for the mark they left in my career and those of a few colleagues: the Kenya Women Finance Trust, now popularly known as KWFT, and the Kenya Rural Enterprise Programme (K-Rep), later known as Sidian Bank. Both organisations were based in Kenya and have since transformed from non-governmental organisations (NGOs) to a microfinance commercial bank and a deposit taking microfinance institution, respectively. In these two organisations, we learnt not only how to love what we did but to love each other and love the clients we served. We became sort of a big extended family. We supported each other and always turned our challenges, especially default collections, into humour. In KWFT, I learnt the basics of micro credit from sales, training, underwriting, monitoring and debt collection all in one job description, a feat only few can dream of. In K-Rep, I learnt the art of reading and interpreting financial statements even though I did not have a finance background. As a branch manager, I had to quickly learn to be an all-rounder, in order to meet the high-performance expectations. Tolerance for mediocrity and errors was low. My branch was 300 KM away from the headquarters, and I had to courier loan application forms two to three times a week for approval by the credit manager, who was as thorough as they come. He would send files back even for a comma being in the wrong place, and this would irritate me thoroughly until I understood that he was mentoring me to be detailed and thorough with everything I did. In later years and to date, I'm grateful to him (may his soul rest in peace), and we remained close until his passing a few years back. Coincidentally, I had worked with him for two years at KWFT. It was not only him who had a habit of detail and timeliness. The managing director was a workaholic. One day, we agreed that he would visit some of my branch clients at 8.00 am on the dot. Driving from about 20 KM away from the meeting venue, I arrived at 8.10 am to find the managing director seated outside the venue, having driven from his station 300 KM away. I was more embarrassed than shocked, but the timely attendance of the clients saved my face that day. He was always a good listener to views and suggestions, but he always had his own set ways and ideas. In K-Rep, the managers, including the branch managers, were exposed to research and consultancy through assignments in other MFIs in various African countries. For that exposure, I will always be grateful, for these were my initial eye-openers regarding the African microfinance movement, and these assignments became my initial self-confidence builders.

Then there were the terrorising K-Rep monthly management meetings where we had to present branch reports both on portfolio performance and profitability, explaining the defaults, actions taken and any deviations from the budget. Those senior managers were merciless, but not in a bad way. They were simply teaching us to be responsible and accountable. The best part was that we all ended up at some 'nyama choma'[1] place after the meeting, where the atmosphere was more relaxed with light moments. We learnt through these interactions that these managers were bosses in the office and at the meetings, but at our social gatherings, we were all equal with no boundaries and no hard feelings. But giving some credit to myself and my two colleagues (Moses, popularly known as Mose or MB, and the late Fred), we took pride in good performance, and we competed healthily against each other. We also played hard together through interbranch visits and games. These two gentlemen as the original branch managers, and me, were like 'The Three Musketeers' of K-Rep. Sometimes to destress, we partied hard after the management meetings, and we always used one car, always driven by Mose, to visit the eateries and drinking places in the city. Mose was our city guide because his branch was in the city. One day we visited a chips and chicken eatery and then walked to a drinking joint in the city centre, but when it was time to go home, we all had forgotten where the car was parked. We believed it was stolen. Mose, after downing a few

---

[1] *Famous Kenyan style roast meats*

tuskers,[2] was adamant that he was standing in the very spot he had parked the car, and the only logical conclusion was that the car had been stolen. As we excitedly debated the incredible theft, we walked down the road, not knowing the next course of action, only to find the car 500 metres ahead. For days we recalled this incident and laughed our heads off. So, we went to work, and we worked hard, but when we went out to play, it was also done with equal commitment.

In K-Rep, there was a zero tolerance for corruption or anything that could be considered a bribe, and every new staff member was welcomed with the slogan, 'Not even a cup of water'. This was so inculcated in us that it would sometimes cause misunderstandings with generous clients who, during business site visits, would offer a bunch of carrots or tomatoes, which we would gently refuse to accept, and if they insisted, we offered to pay for it. This puzzled many clients because, generally, Africans are generous people; if one visits even relatives, they are usually offered a little of the season's produce. So, in the minds of clients, a kilo of carrots or cabbage would not necessarily be a bribe, but in the minds of K-Rep staff, it

---

[2] *Tusker is a famous Kenyan beer*

could be considered some sort of bribe and could compromise one's judgement or decision. Later, clients, especially those selling fresh produce, would joke with each other that, *'Wachana na hawa watu wa K-Rep wanaogopa hongo sana'*[3]. Zero tolerance for corruption was practised by the book, so even whistleblowing was taken seriously. I remember being investigated for an alleged bribe, which I did not commit. The auditors were sent from head office directly to the client, who informed me of the facts after the investigation. The client was so amused by the thought of anyone believing that I of all the branch staff could entertain a bribe, and she said, *'It is a pity your bosses don't really know you the way we do.'* It was not only corruption that K-Rep took seriously, but client or staff abuse, including sexual harassment. Clients and staff could raise complaints if they felt abused in any way. While these were good practices, sometimes underperforming staff and clients could take advantage by raising false complaints. But nonetheless, all complaints were always investigated. I faced a disciplinary committee once for allegations that I was too hard on staff. The performers never had a problem with my

---

[3] *Meaning 'Leave these K-Rep people alone; they are so scared of anything that might be considered a bribe'.*

approach, and they always said, *'TM[4] has no problem if you are performing, but if you underperform, you will face the music.'* They never defined the music. I was also young, about the same age as my staff, a little overzealous on my part and maybe a little jealousy on the part of my staff. On realising that the complaints were based on emotions rather than facts, my supervisors soon left me on my own. I learnt from these events, and I believe I improved my management and leadership style as time passed, and on the whole, I want to believe I delivered on the job.

In the integrated approach, outreach was limited because of the individual or one on one approach. Owners of micro and small businesses accessed loans to expand their businesses after successfully going through one to two weeks of training. As extension officers, we faced tough board credit committees that were composed usually of elderly board members who were often entrepreneurs themselves. In spite of this rigour, the non-performing loans were always a challenge. But we were equally a challenge to defaulters. Some defaulters in my

---

[4] *A short form or the initials of my name. We all referred to one another using the initials of our names.*

branch knew my car registration by heart and confessed that whenever they saw KYR on the road, they would not eat or would be forced to leave their homes at dawn because they knew I would sometimes show up at their homesteads at 6.00 am. Some defaulters would see me at church and leave in a hurry before the end of the service to avoid meeting with me afterwards. On the brighter side, I frequently meet some of my old customers in my original hometown of Eldoret who have done well for themselves and are kind enough to give me and my team partial credit for how their lives have transformed.

During that time or phase of microfinance, the management of information systems, especially regarding credit operations, was basically manual. At the end of every month, credit officers spent long hours reconciling first with the clients and then with the accountants using simple Excel spreadsheets, popularly known at the time as client registers and client passbooks, in which group treasurers kept a weekly record of loans and savings payments. The success of groups was built mainly on initial training, and weekly monitoring through weekly meetings. Clients of that time were less exposed and did as they were told, and this kept the group co-guarantee effective. The group co-guarantee mechanism occasionally broke down because of poor leadership and inadequate supervision. There were also limited but frequent cases of fraud both at credit officer level and also at group treasurer level. Most of these were resolved through 'gentlemen's agreements', but there were always a few cases that required legal action. The legal processes were always slow, and we would try to sort these issues through out of court agreements and settlements, and sometimes with the help of the local police, especially in the fraud cases. But on the whole clients were generally honest. I remember one incident where a client went to the bank to cash out her loan, and instead of paying 10,000, the cashier paid 100,000. On realising the mistake, she panicked and called my office for help to retrieve the excess cash paid to the client. We drove to the client's house and explained the mistake, which she quickly acknowledged and offered to refund the cash. That kind of innocence or honesty has died with the paradigm shifts as clients have become savvier and less trustworthy.

The first paradigm that came in the early nineties was not because of a market need but because the donors got critical about value for money with outreach as a main proxy for measurement. To keep the donor taps open, the microfinance gurus of the time came up with a new approach popularly known as 'the minimalist credit approach'. This was predicated on the belief that small business owners had been in business for years and did not necessarily require training on how to sell tomatoes or 'mandazis' [5]. Neither did 'mama mbogas'[6] require training to do what they had been doing for years successfully. I think the plot got vague because the providers forgot to ask and answer two crucial questions: firstly, why do people start a small business? Secondly, what would the providers be funding, business survival/continuity or growth? In the case of the second question, a follow-up question would have been appropriate: whose survival/continuity and whose growth? The client or the provider, or both. From the institution's perspective, even to date, I suspect the providers do not care much about the survival and growth of the client's business, but the survival and growth of the providers; after all, that is how the sector workers earn and how the gurus made and make their millions off the backs of poor people. The evidence is out there: the number and increase of donors

---

[5] *Mandazis are a form of doughnuts especially popular in East Africa.*

[6] *Swahili word for women selling vegetable in marketplaces*

transforming themselves into lenders and shareholders, while little is reported of business growth and new jobs created, which is partially the essence of supporting small enterprises. I'm being controversial here, but as a practitioner I believe I have the right of opinion, which can be subject to healthy debate by other practitioners and interested parties.

To make a success of the paradigm shift, the African microfinance gurus, including my own managing director, headed to Bangladesh to learn from Mohammed Yunus of the famous Grameen Bank, while others headed to Bolivia to learn from Banco Sol, and soon after, the minimalist credit only approach blossomed in Africa and resulted in unprecedented outreach numbers that could only have been a dream in the integrated approach, and that is because the minimalist approach used a group methodology unlike the individual approach in the integrated system. With such success and with the donor focus on value for money, the providers paid more attention to the need for performance, not only in outreach but in operational and financial sustainability, which were and still are a function of numbers, size of the loan portfolio, portfolio performance and price. Looking at these facts closely, it is clear that the focus was more on the provider, not the client. The providers realised they needed better systems to track and measure these indicators, and this resulted in a significant transformation in the management of information systems, which is still evolving, even today, and something that was only rudimentary in the integrated approach. Numerous existing studies on the minimalist approach show that this approach was superior and yielded quality results, including magic repayment rates of above 95%. The donors were happy, the providers were happy, and they wanted their success stories heard, and because of this, there are many publications out there attesting to these facts. Practitioners published books, the micro-credit summit was created, and the success stories of performing institutions around the world took centre stage, with few client success stories being published. Some of us, with our heads and hearts for the client, sometimes felt a little trapped because our jobs belonged to the providers, and we were just the 'handy boys and girls'.

This went on until the mid-twenties when another shift occurred. This shift ushered in new players, products and services, but the latter remained overall supply centric with lip service to client needs. Unlike the previous shift driven by donors, this shift was driven by the providers who felt frustrated at losing clients to the banks. The microfinance institutions (MFIs) were only dealing in credit, and small loan tickets, yet clients kept asking for bigger loans. With a lot of publicity on outreach and good repayments, it was not long before the commercial banks looked downstream for new customers. While the banks' move downstream was good for the MFI customers, it seemed unfair that MFIs had invested a lot in facilitating a good credit history in micro-credit clients only to lose to banks who had invested nothing. The banks were also advantaged because they did not only have capital but well-established systems. But they had one drawback: they had no knowledge of how to approach or build relationships with micro and small clients, but that did not stop them from moving downstream. Other than MFIs, other stakeholders, including donors, were excited about this shift and out went the minimalist approach, and in came financial inclusion. The MFIs had no choice but to embrace the shift and adapt through the expansion of services beyond credit. Mergers and alliances between MFIs and banks were tried but were not always successful because of the differing institutional cultures and values. Some MFIs went it alone, hence the transformation journey into microfinance banks or deposit-taking MFIs.

Experience has shown that those that have transformed have grown their loan books significantly, but the growth in savings and other services remains marginal compared to the respective loan books. This can be attributed to several factors like concern for clients over the safety of their savings in institutions not known traditionally to deal in savings, but more importantly due to the absence of developed systems within the MFIs that would enable customers to easily access savings at short notice without a long ceremonial process. Overall, the microfinance customer still prefers highly liquid savings, which many MFIs may not offer because one of the reasons for deposit mobilisation to start with was to fund the growth of the loan book, and this can't be done through highly liquid savings. To overcome this drawback, some MFIs have focused on medium to long-term deposits, usually from medium and large institutions. This approach lends validity to my view that it is not really the need of the customer at the core, but the survival of the MFI. The approach of medium to long-term deposits is not only expensive but introduces the risk of concentration, meaning the MFIs are caught between the hard place and the rock. Probably, a good solution would balance the micro customer's need for high liquid savings and medium/long term deposits. This requires creativity and high marketing and sales skills on the part of the MFIs, but these are often missing. Efforts have been made, but these efforts are often disjointed through the different functionalities of the MFIs. Some of the MFIs have found it impossible to drop their culture of credit focus. Credit is so ingrained that any other service is usually looked at from the 'eyes' of credit, which is a pity because great opportunities are missed.

Other than the big market disruption by technology, there have been challenges through the shifts, which include but are not limited to dwindling funds as donor priorities have shifted from microfinance to other sectors such as health and the environment. Even though MFIs have worked so hard to be sustainable, a sizeable number continue to struggle. The group methodology has been heavily people-centred and has contributed to low sustainability. But also, MFIs have not necessarily been the most efficient. Some still run like NGOs and spend heavily with minimal reference to the concept that 'you cannot spend what you don't have'. But one thing that has transformed with the times is the management information system.

During my entry into the market in the late eighties, we kept manual loan disbursement and repayment records, but through the shift, these have been computerised, making it possible to print many records and reports at the touch of a computer button. But whether MFIs have used the reports to improve processes and systems is debatable. I once asked an operations manager of an MFI to explain how they use the analysis report generated monthly, and he was tongue-tied, and after a while, he told me it was part of the board pack. This story I have heard or experienced many times, even with the field staff, who could not explain the concept behind a specific policy, and they take the easy way out by telling the clients, *'It is policy'* or *'Head office requires you to…'.* When a loan application is rejected, the message that goes to the client sometimes is that his or her application has been rejected, but no further explanations as to the reasons are offered. This may mean the quality of staff orientation may have gone down with time, and few MFI staff understand why specific policies are good for both the institution and the client.

Increased competition due to new entrants caught many MFIs unprepared, and they struggled to hold their size of the market. The most dramatic challenge has been the change in client preferences and tastes. The clients now demand more information and insist on the small print being printed in bold. Many clients have lost interest in the group methodology, which has been the MFI signature methodology for over two decades. While the group methodology was one and is still a critical way to reach many people, within short periods, it penalised good payers by making them responsible for bad payers through delay or denial of further services. It would seem like this approach has served its purpose, but the MFIs are still struggling with this reality to date. While some countries and respective MFIs have or are slowly moving away from the group approach, some are stuck and do not know how else they could ever serve the clients without the group system. The clients stepped up and refused to be told what to do and how to do it. They insisted on a partnership approach, where the client should have as much say as the MFI in terms of products, services and how the service is delivered. Many MFIs have struggled with accepting this approach, for they were not used to working with but for the clients. This shows how MFIs were, and many are still not prepared for this change and resulting need for business transformation. Some MFIs and some banks as well have learnt how to serve through groups by collaborating with organised community-based savings and credit groups, while others have adopted a more individual lending approach.

Pictorial view of some of the author's microfinance operations involvements

With colleagues attending a credit officer induction course at my second MFI employer in 1991 in Eldoret, Kenya

With Mose and a colleague in a staff training session in Kenya (1992)

Leading a client training session at my branch in Kenya (1992)

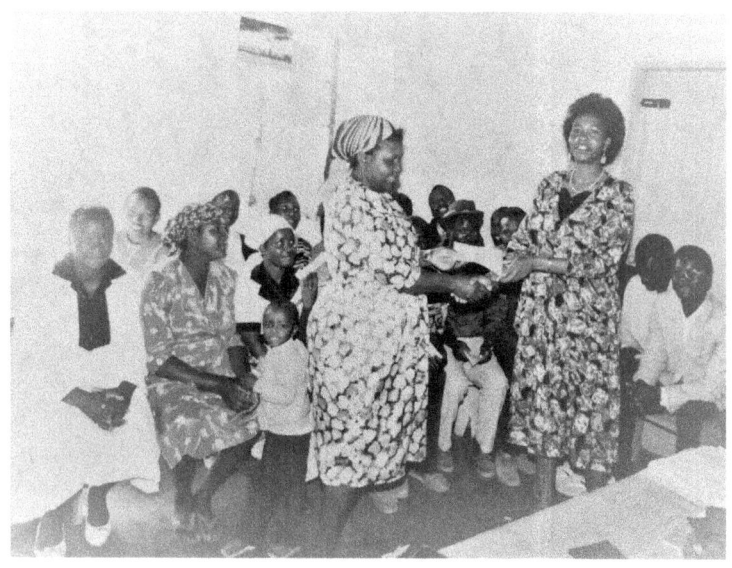

Disbursing loans to clients at my branch in Kenya (1994)

Visiting women farmers and rural entrepreneurs in Zambia (2019)

CHAPTER 2

THE NEW MARKET PLAYERS: WERE THEY BETTER SUITORS?

In giving credit where it is due, the paradigm shifts have not only benefited the players, but the clients as well through increased access and increased choices in product and service offerings. What is debatable is whether the wider choice reflected the actual needs of the clients, the perceived needs or an improvised need? In my consulting work, I have had MSME clients explain to me that they are banking with a particular bank not because the product matches their needs but because of proximity; some banks have agents close to them, so they can save time and money in the banking process. Some clients have explained that they have accessed mobile loans out of desperate need despite the fact that the credit price and size were not right for them. In this case the choices for them were still limited.

There have been new entrants into the sector, pushing and achieving unprecedented outreach results through more effective delivery mechanisms, and this has forced both MFIs and banks to adapt. The positive shifts have not been without challenges, which include tighter regulatory frameworks and risks in general. The new players were initially composed of mainly mobile network operators (MNOs) and were later joined by financial technology companies popularly known as FinTechs. During this period, there was also mushrooming of 'payroll' lenders or consumer lenders (but they did not like to be called consumer lenders) especially coming out of South Africa and expanding into the rest of the Southern Africa region, especially in Malawi and Zambia. These payroll lenders consider themselves another form of MFIs, but they differ completely from the traditional MFIs in mission, target client, pricing, loan sizes and risk exposures. These lenders have polarised the traditional MFI market and contributed to tensions between governments/regulators and the traditional MFIs and have contributed significantly to the introduction or threats of interest rate capping.

In Zambia, several traditional MFIs collapsed as they could not cope with the interest rate cap, and by the time this law was reversed, the damage had been done. Kenya also imposed an interest rate cap for almost two years, and it had nothing to do with payroll lenders but was more politically motivated. But this was also reversed after the realisation that the cap was hurting the same client it was meant to protect: the MSME. Malawi is debating whether to introduce the interest rate cap, and it is not clear how this will end. In Zambia and Malawi, the governments have argued rightly that some lenders have lent irresponsibly, leading to over-indebtedness and increased poverty for the clients through the loss of assets sold to service loans. Some lenders were found to charge up to 200 percent interest per annum, and this, even to the neutral stakeholder, is outrageous. These two governments sent a plea to the lenders to reduce the rates, but overall, such pleas fell on deaf ears. The commercial banks argued that their rates were normal (22% - 27%), and the MFIs justified their rates (about 60%) on the extra risks and unique service delivery, but the consumer lenders were silent. So, it was not surprising that the governments had to intervene in the best way they knew how. The only problem with this intervention was that it was indiscriminate, which meant both the irresponsible and the responsible lenders suffered the same fate. The intervention should have been, or should be, discriminatory because the missions and objectives of these financial institutions differ. Furthermore, they serve different clientele.

The MFIs, for a long time, have had a double-bottom-line mission (financial and social) and some have recently changed to a triple-bottom-line (financial, social and environmental) because of climate change focus. While the banks initially were generally premised on a single-bottom-line, over time they have shifted to a triple-bottom-line, but even then, not with the same intensity as MFIs, as they are still largely guided as single-bottom-line. Both MFIs and banks face high credit risks. The consumer, or payroll lenders, have fewer credit risks because the loans are mostly contingent on an employee's salary and are indirectly guaranteed by the employer, who does direct deductions and forwards payments to the payroll lenders. The focus of payroll lending is mainly motivated by profit. The governments, through their regulators, should take these matters into consideration. It can be argued that the contribution of these institutions to poverty reduction, employment creation and, subsequently, economic development is significantly different as they target people who are already employed. Furthermore, the loans are used mostly for consumption or improving livelihoods.

The MNOs and FinTechs introduced real disruptions and revolutionised financial inclusion. Initially, the focus was on money transfers, which sort of spread like wildfire in Africa, probably because of the way banking was structured based on bricks and mortar and more skewed towards the urban and the more elite clientele. The MNOs and the FinTechs gave a new meaning to banking, where practically every transaction could be done from the comfort of the home or on the go using unstructured supplementary service data (USSD). This has been the most exciting thing that has happened within the sector in Africa in the last decade. It is the most inclusive platform that brought both the young and the old, urban and rural, to the same space. For once, to the ordinary person, it did not matter what the banks did. In Kenya, the banks initially tried to influence the regulator against the wave of mobile money, arguing that the MNOs were introducing a virtual debit card through the back door, but along the way, they lost that argument. But fifteen years later, it emerges that the banks were right, given the examples of Ecocash in Zimbabwe, TNM's debit card in Malawi and Rwanda's MTN preparing to launch. They are providing a similar product like a bank debit card but with softer regulatory oversight. With these examples, the

MNOs collaborate with commercial banks and offer physical debit cards and not virtual, as was/is the case with Safaricom in Kenya.

Unlike banks, the MFIs have struggled to form win-win alliances with MNOs and/or FinTechs, and they have also found it expensive to introduce the MFI led mobile services. On the surface, one would say the struggle has mainly been occasioned by inadequate funding, which led to inadequate systems and inadequate internal capacity. Many are still stuck at the basic digital transformation level. But looking more critically, the MFIs have been inward-looking and continued living in their glorious past. They have also been protective of 'their turf', viewing the bigger players as the villains. The digital wave left many unprepared. Even though the situation has changed for the better in the last few years, the governance structures and hence strategic oversight have been weak, with strong management boards who practically remained a law unto themselves for a long time or accountable to a selectively empowered chairperson while the rest of the board played a 'rubber stamping' role.

That these institutions have often operated with grants and donations also challenged the speed with which they could change their strategic focus, especially where they were dealing with different donors who may have had different interests. The few that have tried partnerships with MNOs have often complained that they had little control of key disbursement/collection processes, marketing and feasibility. The expected conversion of MNO clientele has not happened as expected by some MFIs. The MFIs have had minimum direct control of default management, yet they bear the credit risk exposure. This cannot be blamed solely on the MNOs, as it demonstrates the inadequate capacity on the part of the MFI to foresee risks, mitigate and negotiate better. The big banks, because of their funding bases, have had the luxury of bypassing the MNOs and establishing their own mobile platforms made possible by the standardised application program interfaces (APIs) and the availability of easy to 'plug and play' third-party technologies.

But overall, digital developments have brought about more good than bad for the client, especially with credit, person-to-person (P2P) payments, person-to-business (P2B) payments and business-to-person (B2P) payments. This is for the time being, anyway, because no one is certain about what the future holds. Interestingly, mobile savings has not progressed as much as credit and payments have.

Seeing that they could not beat the new market suitors, the commercial banks acted smart and joined them, which was a clever move because they could still hold the lucrative end of the stick. And because of their more than adequate capital outlay and developed systems, it was easy to integrate digital financial services, inclusive of mobile money, agency banking and both local and international remittances. But the reason for banks jumping onto the bandwagon differs completely from that of MFIs. The banks' adoption of digital finance was mostly to cut costs, improve efficiencies and make more profits, while the former were driven first by the need to increase financial inclusion and subsequently become sustainable.

Mobile money remains by far the most popular of the digital platforms, if the number of annual transactions is anything to go by, while agency banking is increasingly becoming a banking platform of choice for some, especially for rural and peri-urban clients. Agency banking in some countries faced a slow uptake, probably because clients did not have enough trust, nor did they understand how the small point-of-sale devices interacted with their bank accounts in real time. It seemed unreal and appeared some kind of a gimmick to 'steal' their money. Then there arose challenges of liquidity, with some agents forcing clients back into banking halls. Also, power outages and interruptions have discouraged some clients from using agents. The situation is improving, especially with banks moving away from the requirement for exclusivity with agents and the introduction of solar power in many parts of Africa. The entry requirements in terms of capital and structures were and still are within reach for most MSMEs. Those who have ventured into this business have reported good results, albeit with high risks of theft in some countries.

Has digital finance promoted consumerism and created hardened criminals?

But the question that remains is whether the industry has birthed and nurtured opportunists or innovators, especially with FinTechs, which have mushroomed everywhere, with increased fraud and non-performing loans, which goes unnoticed or unreported because it is probably not material compared to the profits being made.

But digital financial services have undoubtedly contributed significantly to financial inclusion, which in turn has resulted in better livelihoods through business investments and cash flow smoothing. The slow growth of mobile savings against the ever-expanding credit culture may suggest there is increased consumable credit rather than asset building.

People are spending beyond their means through various credit methods. Most people who borrow via the mobile platforms do so for quick fixes or emergencies like paying utility or hospital bills and, in some extreme cases, to pay off a threatening money lender. But what is more worrying is that some people are borrowing because the loans are easily available, and they apply the funds to uses that would be termed unnecessary under limited finance access. People are becoming addicted to borrowing, and because often the borrowed amounts are small and easy to access, many borrowers are not necessarily thinking of using these to invest in productive activities but spending and borrowing again. People are being enslaved, especially because good repayment automatically means a higher subsequent loan, and this is tempting. The saving culture is slowly dying, especially with those low in income levels who have been the focus of financial inclusion for decades. Maybe a decade or a few years from now, new programmes and projects will emerge to educate low-income people to get out of debt and re-learn how to save. Meanwhile, the rich are getting richer.

It is not uncommon to find individuals who have borrowed from multiple platforms and some way above their means, leading to poor repayments. There are more people playing 'hide and seek' with mobile lenders, and they don't feel bad that they are becoming bad debtors. Some have borrowed from one mobile platform and because the repayments are set to recoup from the mobile wallet, they decide not to top up the wallet but register a new sim card or use a friend's or a family member's number to receive due payments. Two examples come to mind. Once, a relative requested financial assistance from me, and when I asked her to confirm her mobile number, she told me to send the money to her husband's number because she had a Fuliza[7] loan she could not repay. At the same time, an MFI was going after her to auction her business machines for non-repayment of a loan. What shocked me was the fact she did not seem concerned that

---

[7] *Fuliza is an overdraft service from Kenya's safaricom*

she was trying to evade loan repayments from several lenders.

Also, the Internet is full of stories of how Fuliza subscribers can bypass the system and increase their overdraft limit! Some share stories of how to avoid Fuliza payments. In Malawi, I was talking to high school kids who had perfected the art of borrowing the maximum allowable credit from the MNOs and then skipping the repayment by never topping up their credit and instead requesting parents to share Internet bundles, which they could use for WhatsApp calls instead of the normal telephone line calls. Such loans were/are eventually written off.

While banks did not seem to have suffered the same fate or on a similar scale, some MFIs, MNOs and Fintechs have reported that clients have learnt to ignore calls from their call centres. They can pick up calls the first time and make promises to pay, but after that, they don't pick up, and neither do they keep their promises to pay. They don't care anymore, and no one can make them pay; if the payment occurs, it will probably be on the defaulter's terms.

It is not clear how rampant this behaviour is and how it differs from country to country. But a 2021 report by the Groupe Speciale Mobile Association (GSMA)[8] indicates a big variance between registered accounts and active accounts across the region, and this could lend itself to repayment evasion to some extent, even though there may be many other factors that lead to the dormancy of accounts.

What happened to customer service through the shifts and in the digital transformation?

Throughout the different paradigm shifts, customer centricity within the sector has been here and there and everywhere. It has been one of those highly charged topics but with weak roots. The market has been more supply oriented, especially initially when products and services directly or indirectly favoured the supplier. If and when the customer's interests were discussed, it was more of a 'lip service'. During the time, products and/or services were more of a 'one size fits all', and some clients have related sad stories of how they had suffered at the hands of bad debt collectors or in the attachment of their pledged household or business collaterals by their group members and the lenders' staff. Some clients

---

[8] *Andersson-Manjang. S.K et al: The State of the Industry Report of Mobile Money (www.gsma.com/mobilemoney*

reported that the application process took too long, causing loss of business opportunities, which led to difficulties in repaying loans, yet the institutions would not take any responsibility for subsequent poor repayments. Some credit or loan officers were said to have been outrightly rude to clients, while others failed to educate clients on loan agreements and the resulting penalties if they failed to repay. But a lot of these practices have changed over time for the better.

As best practices evolved, funders, regulators and other stakeholders asked how the client's needs were being met. The institutions themselves became more aware of the need for better client practices, while the clients became more informed and demanded better. With new entrants into the market, the clients now had choices, so the suppliers were forced to consider their needs. With the emergence of the global Smart Campaign led by the Centre for Financial Inclusion (CFI), many MFIs were nudged towards customer centricity. In the last decade, it has been possible to come across more stories of better treatment of clients through education, disclosure and responsible lending. Those who ignore the needs or the voice of the client do so at their own peril. Clients have become more aggressive and more demanding, especially regarding disclosure, turnaround time, responsiveness and responsible pricing. They have made it clear they are not here to play nice but for a win-win collaboration with the financial institutions.

Despite the positive developments, it is not convincing that all suppliers are wholeheartedly practising customer-centricity, because some are yet to develop better client systems, and for some that have done so, the existing client charters are used to tick boxes. But one thing is clear: digital disruption has added more power to the client by making information easily accessible and increasing the choice options. The institutions have been forced to be more transparent and improve turnaround time. But overall, financial institutions have been slow to transform the customer experience, as evidenced by their tendency to offer standardised products and services. There are still too many 'plug and play' kinds of systems or channels, which are too much top down. The other significant observation is that, overall, the providers still expect clients to choose one or the other delivery channel instead of supporting the client's need/s for multiple touch points depending on the unique circumstances at the specific times on the service continuum. For example, one day, a client may need and be comfortable using the mobile platform, but the next day they may need to visit an agent or visit the banking hall. So, the approach should not be 'either or' but 'any of the following' to be used interchangeably according to the convenience of the client, not the convenience of the provider.

MFIs have learnt that marketing is important for business survival; word of mouth and referrals are no longer adequate, yet a lot of it is still lip service mainly because of limited resources. Whenever there is a cut in the budget, the first place MFIs look to is marketing, and because of this, they may continue to suffer negative consequences regarding sales, especially for those mobilising deposits. Banks have continued to do better in this aspect and, directly or through MNO collaborations, have moved into the MFI space. With the current development of digital media, if an institution does not tell its story in the way they want the client to perceive it, someone else will tell the story on their behalf, and if someone else tells the story, there is no guarantee that the perception will always be positive. Even though many people know that not everything reported in the media is to be believed, there is still widespread belief of what people read and hear. On a positive note, the MFIs are participating more in communities through social corporate responsibility activities. They are being more responsive, and take the services closer to the clients, and the staff are more friendly and exert deliberate effort in relating to and helping the clients succeed.

However, in regard specifically to digital finance, many complaints by clients indicate a need for some practices to be improved. For example, there is a need to deal with system hang-ups or upgrades that tend to disrupt services for hours frequently, and during such periods, 'real-time' is not always real, especially for transactions between the bank account and the mobile wallet; money can go missing for days before a reversal is done after several phone calls or an appearance at the banking hall. The client's irritation arises because the banks and MFIs tend to hide behind the MNO poor system and vice versa or the need for reconciliation before a reversal is done. Then there are the agents that usually run into liquidity shortages meaning clients cannot undertake withdrawals when they want to, so time is wasted visiting the agent, then eventually having to go to the MFI banking hall.

Other malpractices reported by clients include the act of mobile lenders involving family members or friends in default collection, yet the family may not have been aware that their kin took a loan. In Kenya, digital lenders have been reported to forward names of defaulters to the credit bureaus for listing. This is done without the authority of the client. The clients say this is embarrassing and breaks the privacy protocol between the lender and the borrower. As for the listing, the regulator has caught up with the digital lenders, as they now must inform the client of the intention to forward their names to the credit bureau.

Then there are the many loan reminder text messages that one can receive in one day. A friend reported that she received five text messages within just five hours, meaning a text every hour, and she paid off the loan and decided never to borrow again. There are other untold stories of how lenders disrupt clients' peace of mind or business activities to ensure the loans are repaid on time. Then there is the automatic sweep of the wallet, which discourages clients from saving, and the many phone calls from call centres. The worst the clients say is the high interest rate, which can be as high as 10% per month. When Kenya and Zambia effected interest rate caps, the mobile loans remained unaffected because the lenders claimed they don't charge 'interest', but 'fees and commissions', but for practical purposes that kind of explanation is so political. Other ills that face both clients and agents are risks of fraud and theft.

CHAPTER 3

SO MUCH TALK ABOUT GOOD GOVERNANCE PRACTICES

Precepts of governance

According to the United Nations Educational, Scientific and Cultural Organization (UNESCO) International Bureau of Education, governance embodies *'accountability, transparency, responsiveness, rule of law, stability, equity and inclusiveness, empowerment and broad-based participation'*[9] through properly defined structures and processes.

While the precepts of governance are similar for all organisations, whether private, public or non-state agents/ non-governmental organisations (NGOs) or MFIs, differences arise in practice. While private organisations focus largely on the achievement of financial returns and shareholder value, most MFIs focus on the achievement

---

[9] *www.ide.unesco.org/en/gegaf/technical-notes/concept-governance*

of a 'double' bottom line: financial returns and social responsibility, but in recent years, there has been a great push for a 'triple' bottom-line, which incorporates environmental responsibility. The duties and responsibilities of directors across the different types of organisations remain similar. The majority of organisations supporting or promoting financial inclusion and/or supporting MSMEs are largely NGOs or companies limited by guarantees, and traditionally these organisations have not had strong governance structures or processes for the longest duration, because the selection of board members was based on personal relationships rather than knowledge and skills. But this has changed over time, as more MFIs now attempt to focus more on knowledge, skills and experience in recruiting their boards[10].

Transforming the governing mindset

Traversing East, South and sometimes West Africa, I have seen and experienced both incredible and mediocre efforts by MFIs to facilitate the transformation of MSMEs by improving access to finance. Some MFIs have done better

---

[10] *http://aicd.companydirectors.com.au/resources/all-sectors/roles-duties-and-responsibilities/governance-of-not-for-profit-organisations?no_redirect=true*

than others, and success is usually defined by outreach and sustainability. It is ironic that there is little attempt or information regarding the sustainability of the MSMEs themselves despite millions being invested, either through grants or equity investments. Impact studies are probably far in between. Also, for every success, there is probably equal institutional failure that goes unreported. Both success and failure can be attributed to many things, and proper governance or the lack of it will be somewhere on top of that list. Some great work has been done and continues to be done to ensure more unserved people access resources, including finance.

Now we are living in exciting times in respect of technology, and I smile thinking about an article I wrote several years ago, titled '*Warning to Microfinance Institutions in Africa: Innovate or Die*', which was published in the *Enterprise Development & Microfinance* journal[11]. We are now living in that space, and it is not like I was a prophet or anything like it, but anyone who was intrinsically involved with the sector then would have

[11] *Enterprise Development & Microfinance*
An international journal
Twentieth anniversary edition
Volume 20 Number 4 (December 2009)

seen where it was headed. Those who refused to change have died a natural death or have been left by the wayside, struggling, with little chance of survival. This includes both institutions and practitioners. The latter have been better at adapting. For those still debating the good of technology, Covid-19 travelled across borders without invitation or passport and helped to fast track the conviction to embrace technology or become irrelevant. Without warning and time to prepare, many were forced to go digital in most aspects of their operations, and the boards were no exception. For eight years until 2020, I attended physical board meetings and never imagined a board would succeed in its operations through virtual meetings, but the emergence of Covid-19 left us with no option. For the last two years, our board has met virtually and performed even better, not only in attendance but in dealing with strategic institutional issues, communication and response rate, and opportunities to make substantial savings.

For over thirty years, I have been involved with micro, small and medium enterprises (MSMEs) within East and Sothern Africa through credit operations, training, capacity building, project design, project supervision and project evaluation. I have basically grown up professionally in the sector and witnessed a fundamental transformation from integrated approaches to minimalist credit, microfinance and the current era of financial inclusion first hand. I have come from the field into management, then into the boardroom. The field and management of lending operations sort of prepared me for the boardroom, and while that background has given me a competitive edge as a board member, it has also tested my abilities to delineate governance best practices from those of management. In my experience, the former has outweighed the latter. In my board life, I have met only two other members who brought the same versatility, and I was always grateful to them because it meant I did not have to read and critique every document by myself as a chairperson. But I also observed two colleagues experience similar struggles like me, sometimes losing themselves in too much operational detail at the expense of the bigger picture.

One frustration I have encountered both as a board member and a chairperson are members who attend meetings unprepared and always wait for others to comment or propose before happily endorsing. Such members never lead in anything and are usually limited in critiquing the strategic focus or management performance.

Such members are also not good at attending meetings or going the extra mile when circumstances require them to do so. They are usually like joy riders or outsiders on the inside. To some extent, such membership may arise due to poor recruitment practices, poor orientation and lack of training and development. Even though these processes have improved over time, they still leave a lot to be desired, especially in training and development. It is often assumed that because many board members are professionals, they do not require training, but this is far from the truth because each institution is unique in focus, culture and strategic alliances. Some of the new members are retired from their professions, and to them, board membership is like a hobby that does not require too much effort. While the retired members bring to the table many years of experience, they often lack the initiative and drive required. Poor leadership, especially by the chairperson, can also contribute to the non-performance of the board in general.

The boardroom politics and alliances

Until I experienced it first-hand, I used to think that boardroom politics was unduly exaggerated. One may ignore the power of politics at their own risk. First, there usually occurs a divide between the independent directors and the executive directors because while the former tries to represent all stakeholders, the latter are mainly interested in the shareholder. There may also be times that the shareholder's interests may not always be aligned with the regulations or even staff interests. For example, the shareholder rightly expects dividends, while staff may demand better remuneration packages, yet the profitability levels may not always support all these demands, and the board has to make a judgement call or practise some balancing acts. The management board may be forced in such circumstances to realign with the executive directors on the assumption that the security of their jobs depends on this group. From my experience, this is a wrong assumption because, in a proper functional board, a majority vote is needed for any resolution to be binding.

Small informal groupings or alliances may occur based on personal relationships within and outside the board. These small groups discuss and agree on a stand on specific issues before the official board meeting. This would result in long deliberations, fewer resolutions and more extra meetings. The board may become ineffective. Such groupings are not necessarily bad all the time but can be used to benefit the board if the chairperson plays his or her role well by directing such energies into more positive and objective discussions, which result in definite and amicable resolutions. There are members who may be perceived as even more powerful than the board chairperson because of their connections with shareholders. It takes maturity for such members not to bring up their connections in the boardroom. But a good board charter and good leadership can also help neutralise such negative energies.

Even though I have not experienced information leakage on a significant scale, it exists where members with shareholder connections want to influence certain decisions, for example, who gets recruited to the board. They may also leak information regarding management performance, or the performance of individual board members, and influence the shareholder's view. While other members may be renewed for subsequent terms, others may be dropped after only one term or even before their term is over, based on informal evaluation of members. To minimise the negative effects of information leakage or informal evaluation, the chairperson should facilitate open discussions by allocating each member time to speak, undertake an open vote and ensure accurate minuting of proceedings. The chairperson could also try to lobby and get the buy-in from perceived 'troublesome' members regarding the need for both multiple and joint responsibility. This matter can also be managed under the conflict-of-interest declarations, and the code of conduct.

The tenets of a functional board

Understanding governance challenges

The importance of a functional board cannot be overstated, especially during these digital times, because of the challenges faced by pro-financial inclusion organisations. Covid-19 and digital transformation aside, some other key challenges faced by these organisations include inadequate funding, or lack of affordable funding, poor strategic choices, limited capacity and negative political influences, among others[12]. A functional board should consider the organisation's strategic focus and respective knowledge and competencies, the right size to ensure diverse and inclusive participation and control, some independence, especially where the organisation is a subsidiary but locally constituted. Having the right size and competence is just one part of the equation. The other

---

[12] *http://www.penkenya.org/UserSiteFiles/public/*
challenges%20and%20opportunities%20facing%20NGOS.pdf

part is properly organised meetings and attendance, proper records of proceedings and follow through of action points. The glue that will hold the two parts together is sound leadership in the form of the chairperson.

The role of the chairperson

In my experience as a chairperson for the last four years, I have learnt that the chairperson can make or break the integrity of the board. My 'must dos' for every chairperson include consistent and productive interactions with the chief executive officer (CEO) and the legal counsel for advice and guidance on matters requiring the board's immediate attention, keeping the members in the loop regarding developments, drafting meeting agendas, arranging for meetings; ensuring recruitment of new board members is based on the missing competencies or knowledge/skill gaps; ensuring the composition of board sub-committees is based on competencies; facilitating healthy inclusive debates at and outside the meetings and learning not to respond to every commentary; ensuring proceedings are documented accurately through a summary of issues, action points and resolutions; and ensuring the board is held accountable through regular attendance of meetings, participation and performance evaluation. The board chairperson should be observant, a good listener and be able to read both the print and between the line messages in order to hear what is not being said verbally. He/she should ensure every member has an equal chance to share views and ideas, even if it means encouraging or reaching the not-so-outspoken ones outside of official meetings. The idea is to build a consensus or joint responsibility without losing the individuality or independent thinking of members. The board needs to have intermittent contact with staff and clients to avoid the CEO representing himself/herself to the board on the one hand and to the staff on the other hand. The message to the board and staff, and subsequently, to clients, should be aligned, and the chairperson ensures this happens through the human resources board committee. The objective is to create a harmonious environment for progressive growth.

The board charter

A proper functional board is usually guided by a board charter, which stipulates the roles and responsibilities of the board individually and jointly. The charter is a useful tool for training new members, and it also serves as a point of reference if there arises ambiguity during discussions. The charter ideally covers four broad areas: i) key functions, which basically comprise oversight of operations including strategic direction, decision making, compliance and communication; ii) roles that comprise the role of the board, structure, role of members, role of the chairperson, the role of the legal counsel and role of the CEO; iii) board performance, which comprise selection, induction, remuneration, development, evaluation; iv) process and management, which comprise meetings, agenda, meeting calendar and documents. While the draft charter may be drafted by the legal counsel, this should be reviewed and approved by the board and may require an annual review to make sure it remains up to date. The charter is a good point of reference and a good training tool, but it is not common to find that in many institutions where it exists, it is usually forgotten after onboarding.

Recruitment of new board members

The cornerstone

This could be the single and most important cornerstone, yet in my experience, it still lacks objectivity in regard to competence diversity. Personal connections still play a greater role, especially when directors are not independent. Also, where the CEO is stronger than the board, he/she singularly may decide who joins the board. But with regulated institutions, the central bank may critique and recommend recruitment of diverse skills during supervision visits. Sometimes, the shareholder or a lender may impose an advisory member, and this is both good and bad practice; good because such members may come with specialist knowledge and skill, and bad because it may interfere with the board chemistry and the proper functioning of the board. It is important to ensure that there is no disconnect between the boardroom and operations.

Identifying the right competencies

When an opening occurs, the board should ideally review and agree on what knowledge/skill they are missing, so the search or advertisement is developed to attract the missing talent. While many microfinance institutions are still not strictly formal in the board recruitment process, it is advisable to follow the formal process regardless of the approach (advertisement or headhunting). The board itself is a good place to start because they know the market, they know people and they know what is required. It is good to identify at least two to three candidates to be interviewed by the board, who will then make a recommendation to the shareholder/shareholder's representative for approval and appointment. The involvement of the board is important to ensure not only the right competence is recruited but someone with the right attitude and potential to align with culture and chemistry. This process differs from the private and public sector where the board members are solely recruited by the shareholders or the government without the involvement of the existing board members.

The candidates

Some countries are more advanced than others and will not face problems finding the people with the right competencies. Furthermore, the more generic competencies like accounting, audit, legal etc. may be easier to fill. What remains a challenge, in my experience, especially in countries where financial inclusion is less developed, is finding people who understand the business operations, and therefore even when individuals are highly competent in their field, they may not be productive at the board because they will take time to contextualise their knowledge and skills in line with microfinance operations. In such situations, the search may be extended regionally or internationally but within regulatory boundaries.

Managing stakeholder relations is important, yet this skill rarely comes ready-made, it must be developed through exposure and training. The board composition should consider this aspect in addition to the usual business, and not assume that those with experience in the usual business will be able to take care of the shareholder, staff interests and other key stakeholders such as the government, the regulator and the funder. Having people within the board who can easily reach and hold relevant conversations with these stakeholders is useful.

Holding the board accountable for their responsibilities

Many MFIs do not know how to hold the boards accountable, while some boards do not want to be held accountable, as they would rather operate within the grey areas. Accountability starts from identification and recruitment, which should be open and transparent. Once recruited, the members should be trained on their mandates, responsibilities and the general code of conduct. The chairperson should monitor the engagement and contribution of members in meetings and the turnaround time of the approval requests and queries. The charter defines specific parameters that can be used for monitoring and giving feedback to the members.

Training of the board has not been a strong point of many MFIs, probably because of limited resources, but training and development of the board is important, especially where gaps or weaknesses are identified or where there are too many disruptions in the environment. A strong board will hold itself accountable and ensure the growth of the institution. Training does not need to be expensive. It can be done even internally by sharing local and regional sector developments, literature and debates or by attending relevant webinars. The board should be encouraged to be proactive in updating their knowledge and participating in sector events.

The other way to hold the board accountable is through periodic evaluation, which should preferably be done by an external body in order to provide a high level of comfort and candour. Evaluation results should not be traced to specific members as this may create conflict, mistrust and division. While this is the ideal process, it is not certain that it is widely practised except in those MFIs that are regulated, and the regulator insists on board evaluation. The bigger question is what happens after the evaluation, and in my experience, nothing much other than ticking the boxes for the regulators and investors. This is a real missed opportunity to identify gaps and provide practical training and development, which could lead to more effective boards.

Then there is the question of board remuneration, which is a touchy subject, almost taboo amongst the traditional microfinance players. Usually, many MFIs still ride on the 'how we are helping the poor' mentality of the past, and members are expected to volunteer. If anyone dares raise the issue of proper board remuneration, he/she may be looked at as not having a 'heart' for the sector or, worse, as being a traitor. Out of the ten years I was on the board, the first four years were on a voluntary basis. In the MFIs that offer some remuneration by way of a sitting allowance or stipend, as others like to call it, what is offered is sometimes way below the market standards. But the irony is that many MFIs have transformed, with some making good profits and paying dividends to shareholders. The question that may be asked is why is it befitting to pay dividends and not compensate the people who provide oversight for the dividends to happen? It is not surprising therefore that some MFIs may find it difficult to hold the boards responsible, or in some cases the boards don't feel obligated to be accountable, for in their minds, the management gets paid, and management should be accountable for the institutional results. This issue of compensation may also explain in part why some organisations may find it difficult to attract competitive members but instead have a 'rubber stamping' board that is not effective in its overseeing role and leads to stagnation in growth and transformation.

Receiving my board fellowship certificate (Cape town, 2019)

CHAPTER 4

THE WEAK LINK IN THE PARADIGMS

Where to begin

Where does one begin to discuss the state of human capital within the paradigm shifts? Is it their availability, competencies, experience or capacity or ability to adapt? During my career in the early nineties, there were no issues of availability or adaptability. We may have had limitations with competencies and maybe initial challenges in capacity, but these were overcome with a production assembly kind of training. And we also prided ourselves that our hearts and minds were in the right place, and with that, there was nothing we could not achieve once we agreed on targets. We practically worked with the lowest compensation packages and were just happy to see client numbers increase. We were also most excited about lending and attaining high repayment rates consistently. We were sticklers for detail, and we were 'handy' men and women. We were not afraid to walk long distances or to be found in some slum areas, marketing loans. Such was the life of integrated credit and microfinance. When the shifts occurred, we got actively involved in the debates for and against, and if the new shift was something we did not believe in, we moved on happily but remained genuine ambassadors for the sector wherever we went. We were loyal to our employers. This situation was more common in East Africa than in the other parts of the continent. But overall, there was unison between the institutions and the donors on the one hand and institutions and the staff on the other hand.

Then came the sleek boys and girls of the noughties, very gifted in talking, the spoilt kids of microfinance who did not like to get their hands dirty. They wanted to compare themselves with the white-collar boys and girls, and they liked the hype but not the work. Their minds were in the right place, but their hearts were always wondering. In a way, they were like nomads, moving from one institution to another in search of greener pastures. To them, the grass was always greener on the other side, and the concept of loyalty was, to them, very abstract. They were also a bit rough with clients. The external factors did not make the situation better for this lot; the clients became more informed, more vocal and more aggressive, while the donors grumbled about performance and sustainability, and the equilibrium between them and the institutions was disturbed. The institutions, on their part, increased the pressure on the staff, and this increased restlessness and nomadism. To cut costs, there was less training and less focus on staff development. At this point, it became survival of the fittest, and the institutions became less responsible for ensuring that staff moved along the continuum of the paradigm shifts smoothly. It became 'everyone for himself, and God for all of us'.

Too many 'plug and play' systems

As the shifts occurred, the institutions were more focused, if not obsessed, with system upgrades, and they could spend a couple of hundred thousand dollars to upgrade but did not have the money to upgrade the people. People had to fit into whatever systems were being introduced, never mind if these were misaligned. There was too much 'plug and play' going on, and people sometimes felt like square pegs being forced to fit into round holes. The irony of it was that the people were supposed to manage and maintain the systems, so it would make business sense to invest as much in people as in systems. Where training occurred, it was too generic to be applied, it was the 'good to know' kind of knowledge. This is probably because the identification of training needs was never streamlined.

The training and development function was not aligned with operations and was more of an outlier to be referred to at the convenience of a few people within the institution. I remember being part of a project in East Africa that trained a couple of thousand staff within the banking and the MFI sub-sectors, and before any training, we would sit with the institutions to undertake a rapid appraisal and identify key focus areas for training. As we moved from institution to institution, the story remained the same. There was actually no storyline for the training function; it was rather a small dot lost in the big scheme of operations. It seemed like the institutions committed to the training just to tick the lender's box. However much we discussed and promoted the need for monitoring of training effectiveness, the partner institutions did not pay too much attention, and soon after the training, it was business as usual. But to be fair, all was not really lost because, in the last few years, I have come across some people I trained who testified that the training had improved their work process and ethics, but such positive feedback remained with the staff and never got documented at the institutional level.

Sabotaging the change process

Introducing and managing changes was mostly a top-down approach, and while the top understood the logic behind the change, the down was mostly mechanical. They moved along because they were told to do so, and sometimes because they did not understand the logic, they were afraid or became insecure and sabotaged the changes. As part of completing a board training session, which I attended a couple of years back, we were tasked to visit clients of our organisations and develop short case studies to share with peers. As I talked to clients, I was shocked at what I learnt, that even though the institution had introduced individual loans and encouraged group clients to graduate to access bigger loan amounts, some clients reported that they had been advised by their relationship officers not to graduate because at the individual level 'things' would be more difficult and the possibility of getting a loan would be significantly reduced. This information was not true, but the clients had believed and refused to graduate from groups. On interviewing the relationship officers, they reported that they were afraid they would lose clients whom they had recruited and managed over the years, and when I explained how the graduation process worked, they were surprised that they would not lose anything and that in fact they would gain by having more clients graduate. This was a classic case of pushing down the change and ignoring the logic. I discovered that in many institutions, communication of changes was done through a mix of meetings and scanty memorandums. Where verbal communication was used, the message would be lost in translation, and it would not be surprising to find variations of the policy or process in different branches.

It is a pity because these relationship officers were and are the front face of the institutions, they interface with the clients, and because the logic part of the change was or is ignored or downplayed, unlike in the banking sector that carries the clients along the change continuum, the MFIs moved ahead and left the clients and the public behind. This is why there exists some good work done across the continent, but few people get to hear about it. This situation is made worse by the fact that as Africans, we are good at telling stories orally, but not documenting them. We carry a lot of knowledge and experience in our minds but hardly get motivated to share it with the world, which is partly the reason for this book, to encourage others to share their stories so our people can learn and be better.

The failed human resource function

The most frustrating occurrence I have come across are institutions that have had or have ceremonial human resources departments with no capacity or power to transform anyone or anything. Instead of being the leader of change, they were simply the followers of change. This human resource function was more aligned to routine processes like recruitment advertisements, policy training, facilitating annual staff appraisals and some public relations functions. Even in recruitment, the power to hire was always with someone else, but when trouble arose, everyone expected human resources to pull out the magic wand. They were never involved, and neither did they initiate the big picture issues, like defining human resource strategic direction or how human resource capacity could be enhanced to align with the strategic direction. They appeared like 'joy riders' getting paid moderately to undertake simple tasks while the people who did the hard work got paid peanuts. Many human resource heads I came across in my work were technically competent in their subject matter but had limited depth with the core microfinance and functions related to the core business, like risk and financial management. The sad thing about this was and still is that the institutions did not see this as a weakness. In one assignment I undertook, I was at a branch of MFI to discover how the new changes were being rolled out, and in less than twenty minutes, I had gathered that the staff were not opposed to the changes but were rather unhappy about the modalities of the changes, and when I asked them whether they had given feedback to head office, they affirmed that they had talked to their line manager who simply told them that others had signed up to the new approach and targets, so they should sign up and stop complaining. I was shocked at the answer because something was not right with the approach, and it required finetuning with the people who would implement it. In another branch, I learnt that staff were dissatisfied with salary adjustments, but they did not know who to talk to as the head of human resources had responded that the rate of increase was a joint agreement with other senior managers! If the head of human resources could not deal with such queries, where would staff turn to? On whether staff could use the company suggestion boxes or the provided hotline to give feedback, they said they did not trust those systems as the answers could easily be traced back to their computers or to them. In this situation, I concluded there was a problem with communication between the head office and branches, yet the head office was certain everything was going well.

One function that seemed to suffer significant capacity limitations was middle management, which ideally should be the engine of the institution. Many MFI middle managers were and are still homegrown or promoted from within, and this has led to the weak middle, where one finds highly skilled and knowledgeable people in operations but with little exposure to other functional areas such as finance, risk marketing and stakeholder engagement. Because of this, they tend to overcompensate in operations management and neglect the other functions. As a former middle manager, myself, I know this to be a critical position, sort of a middle anchor. These managers are expected to represent senior management, clients and staff all at the same time. In a way, they are the 'jack of all trades and masters of none'. To serve effectively, these managers would need exposure and training, but the MFIs have not had the time nor adequate resources to do so, leading to continued mediocre branch performance in various MFIs. For the regulated MFIs, this is changing because of the requirements imposed by the regulator.

The institutions were not to blame completely for the above state of affairs, because the generation of staff including the Millennials and Generation Z were and are filled with their own wisdom to be completely trainable. They believe too much in their own rights, and a little bit of hard work to them may be interpreted as abuse or a danger to their mental health. Such staff tend to know everything, and to them, learning belonged in the corridors of school and college. They came, they saw and they conquered, and they lack ambition and like easy things. They always have one or the other explanation for poor performance. The most common excuse I have heard is the difficulty of the area of operation or the poor-performing economy, which made it difficult for clients' businesses to grow, or repay their loans on time or save frequently. Listening carefully to the list of excuses, I always wondered why everything seemed external and had nothing to do with 'me'. Until people accept that they don't know or that they are their own worst enemy, they will not become better. And that is still the ill of some MFIs.

However, perhaps if the human resource institutional systems were working as they should have, and the institutional cultures were strong, there would be no reason for these staff to remain in the institutions for years delivering the minimum with a lot of lip service. Unlike the private sector, the MFIs do not espouse strong professional values, and where values exist, this may be merely on paper rather than in practice. In this sector, unprofessional conduct could be excused or left unnoticed on the pretext of relating to the client 'we serve'. I'm of the opinion that relating to the client can be done professionally. The majority of the staff seemed to have transitioned into their own parallel world where they expect improved remuneration despite poor performance, and they often fail to see the effects of the external changes on their institutions and their jobs. In some countries, it is possible to find staff who have changed jobs for a miserly increase of $20; loyalty is no longer a virtue. It would seem that as time has progressed, candidates sought jobs from the sector primarily for money. The concept of the mind and heart being in the right place had been completely forgotten.

Then there has been the category of staff who have fought hard to be sent on different courses within their countries or outside. But their motivation was not to come back and improve the institutional systems or client service but to enhance their resumes. From the project evaluations I have participated in, I have had the opportunity to interact with staff who could not recount even one thing that changed after the training, let alone remember the topics covered. Some of these staff have been more excited to share where they went for training, and the organisers of the training and the certificates they obtained. But the staff were not entirely to blame as some of the training was theoretical and generic, sometimes taught by people who had never worked in the field for a day, so people always went away with information, but not how to implement it. After training, monitoring was and still is rare in many institutions.

In many MFIs, the different departments have tended to operate independently, not appreciating how each department affects the work of the other or how some departments are anchors without which the institutions could not move or grow. It seemed like there has been so much focus on credit operations and finance at the expense of other departments. This has reduced not only the holistic functionality of the institutions but also constrained growth as the departments pulled in different directions. The most common pull I have experienced is between operations and risk on one hand, and operations and audit on the other hand. Even within operations, it is not uncommon to experience tensions between the sales team and the underwriters. While the former view the client with their hearts, the latter view the client from a risk exposure perspective.

A few years back, while training staff of a bank on credit risk management, tensions between these two groups ran so high within the first hour of the training, my co-facilitator and I had to take the next hour to referee, calm emotions down and make the two groups understand they had the same objective, which was to serve customers in the best way possible at the minimum risk. Our advice to them was that the salespeople, while having empathy with the client, should care as much about minimising credit risk exposure and vice versa. In similar regard, the departments often failed to see or realise that they all had the same objective, to be achieved through the different functions. In the boardroom, I often experienced instances where I was forced to arbitrate between the auditors and the management board regarding audit findings. While the audit function should have been welcomed with open arms, it was often seen as inconvenient policing that caused more harm than good.

But in my view, through internal audit, the institutions could and can improve their systems and processes tremendously.

From experience I have tended to blame interdepartmental dysfunctions on chief executive officers because the buck had to stop with someone. Some chief executive officers have ruled not from a level of competence but from power and authority, and this often put fear in their teams and they therefore missed the opportunity to bring the team together to improve or manage changes. Even though this situation would exist whether the chief executive was local or not, it was worse with foreign chief executives because some were culturally insensitive, resulting sometimes in toxic work environments.

As already mentioned, marketing and training departments have been the most neglected on the block, both by design and by default. By design, because of limited resources, and they do not generate revenue directly, and by default, because they were not priority areas. Though there are notable changes in the way departments interact, it is still a slow process.

CHAPTER 5

THE FUNDING TRANSFORMATION

During the first two shifts, MFIs operated basically on grants, which at the time were easy to come by because microfinance was trending, and everyone wanted a piece of the action then. The MFIs needed to demonstrate that they were reaching the 'poor' or the 'bottom of the pyramid'. It was possible for an MFI to have multiple donors at a time, and funding was provided for both operations and loan capital. Life for the MFIs was easy, and the only complaint was the different reporting formats for the different donors. After the nineties, the donations and grants dwindled for reasons highlighted in the earlier sections. Many MFIs explored opportunities for loans and equity as opposed to donations and grants. This has not been an easy road for many because both lenders and investors have stringent qualifying criteria, for example, the need to be regulated by the central bank, a track record of profitability and a portfolio at risk below 10%. Only some of the transformed MFIs could meet such a criterion, while the vast majority of the MFIs are still struggling and continue seeking donations and grants. But in regard to equity funding specifically, some of the transformed MFIs have not been transparent about how the initial donor funds turned into equity for a few top individuals, while the majority of the staff and clients who contributed to the success were left out. Looking critically, the founders have benefited more than any other group of stakeholders. Maybe they were in the right place at the right time, or they were just self-seeking using the poor to enrich themselves. But self-seeking or not, the water already went under the bridge and flowed downstream.

In my interactions with some of MFI CEOs in East and Southern Africa, they have experienced more lending than equity investments. In their view, most loans and equity still come from foreign donor/government institutions, and these are still mainly focused or interested in social impact. Because most of these funds come from taxpayers the application is very controlled. Most funders stipulate that the loans are to be used for lending to deserving sectors, and sometimes they predetermine the sectors. Sometimes, the loans come with technical services directed at either operations or governance or both. When the funders choose the equity approach, it is for a limited period, like five years, after which they sell off their stake. The periodical equity supports the institutions to stabilise operations and attain self-sufficiency. Most foreign loans are free of collateral and are preferred by most MFIs, but the forex exchange risks are higher. Local commercial loans are also available and are generally free of market risks, but the need for collateral is a big hindrance for many institutions. The need for collateral by local lenders is a regulatory requirement based on the Basel Framework[13]. One CEO was of the opinion that it is more challenging to manage foreign loans than local loans, not only because of the forex risk exposures but stringent reporting guidelines and penalties in case of breach of covenants. Whether a foreign or a local loan, the institutions undergo a due diligence process to determine their suitability and their capacity to borrow and repay.

However, the shift to loans and equity is not all glamourous. First, the requirements are stringent, which means only a few institutions can qualify. For example,

---

[13]*The Basel Framework is an internationally agreed set of measures for banking supervision in response to the financial crisis of 2007-2009*

some requirements are far-fetched for the small MFIs. Such requirements may include low portfolio at risk, a track record of profitability, and regulation by the central bank.

It is not uncommon to find multiple lenders or shareholders concentrating on one successful MFI, while the struggling ones attract no funding. In a way, it is the market at play, for no investor wants to invest in an institution that does not promise a fair return, either economically or socially. Some lenders lend in foreign currency, and hedging increases the finance costs eventually. Some MFIs have argued that to continue to serve the poor, there is still a need for some grants to help them undertake research and introduce new technology. Left on their own, they argue these interventions will take longer. They may be tempted to focus on the able clients to increase profitability at the expense of the micro clients.

Despite the challenges, there are still good reasons why MFIs should continue to pursue the long road of loans and equity. First, this approach has assisted in building stronger institutions because the going concern principle is more definite, with proper planning and budgeting. There are fewer breaks in funding, unlike in donations and grants, in which funding is never guaranteed. The institutions are forced to be more strategic in their investments, focus on profitable sectors and delivery mechanisms and hence their potential to become more efficient increases. Donations and grants usually have a short focus and are tied more to purpose and target than sustainability. The former gives the institutions the chance or power to pursue their own agenda aligned to their local circumstances, and not the agenda of the donors who may have bigger agendas for global good and are not necessarily aligned to the local circumstances or the environment. For example, during the early shifts, there was a tendency to focus more on women, regardless of cultural circumstances. Women in some regions or cultures had no ambition to grow businesses beyond the micro level because of family care responsibilities. They wanted businesses that could be managed with less stress, with flexible opening and closing times. But because the institutions were interested in growth they pushed or encouraged women to take bigger loans than they could manage, which sometimes led to defaults. The other example is the focus on youth or agriculture without understanding the historical school systems in Africa, which prepared students for office jobs. The youth would easily abandon the small business for better-paying jobs in cities or neighbouring countries at the slightest sign of challenge. I remember attending a meeting in one of the South African countries to discuss the evaluation results of some projects, and it was clear from the discussion that even the government officials did not believe or agree to mass enterprise training or encouraging communities to upgrade to commercial livestock because they argued it was not an internal need within these special groups. They were critiquing the basis for the project purpose. These circumstances are changing now as more women and youth are getting involved in progressive small businesses voluntarily.

The shift to loan and equity funding is a demonstration of the need to grow and be independent by some institutions. The move also improves corporate governance because of the diluted stockholding by one or two shareholders. More shareholders mean a diversified board that increases transparency and accountability. There is an increased opportunity for professional growth and brand improvement through regulatory oversight, which does not exist in NGOs operating with grants and donations. While the donors did require reports, they were never as stringent as the central banks are, so the likelihood of funds abuse was higher in the early shifts. It was not surprising to find NGO chief executives who grew rich during their period in office from high salaries and a host of allowances. A bit of pilfering on the part of these CEOs could not be ruled out. The irony in such situations was that the people directly responsible for outreach and lending got paid peanuts, while the loans to clients were tiny. It is not surprising therefore that some sceptics have wondered whether microfinance was meant to help the poor or to help the profession. It was even worse during the early days when donor funds were attached to conditions such as technical assistance, which meant over fifty of the donations went back to donating countries in salaries, stipends and consultancy fees. While some of these ills have improved over time, the salary disparities still exist, even to date, but there is a better balance between the external and the internal customer.

Also, with this shift from grants to loans and equity, there has been a tendency for MFIs to view each other as competitors, resulting in fewer collaborations, leaving room for the defaulters to crisscross the market freely, especially in markets where the credit reference bureaus do not exist or are not functional. This also means minimum sharing of information and experiences, hence wastage of resources through 're-inventing of the wheel'.

CHAPTER 6

REGULATION IN THE PARADIGMS

While writing this book, I had a discussion with three acquaintances, and one of them had been a staff of the regulator in his country for the whole of his career. When I asked them how the regulation of microfinance had changed in the last two decades, the one who had worked for the regulator was surprised by the question because, according to him, other than the law enacted, nothing much had happened. At first, I laughed, thinking his answer was a joke, but then I realised he was serious. He even forgot to mention that regulating MFIs was a major shift during these two decades. I was taken aback and wondered if I had overrated the regulatory changes within the shifts. But then, the other two acquaintances mentioned several highlights, which included the introduction of microfinance and financial inclusion policies and strategies, which paved the way for the introduction of microfinance laws and regulations. They also mentioned that other than the new laws, new regulations had been introduced because of new players, especially regarding digital payments and money transfers.

In spite of the new laws, innovation and new players have always seemed to run ahead of regulation, especially in East Africa, where new entrants seemed to escape regulation for over a decade. Even the briefcase or the mobile ones thrived and disrupted the level playing field for traditional players. In Kenya, the digital lenders, after having funded anonymity entrance into the market for over a decade, now must furnish the regulator with the source of funding. According to the regulator, this is to curb incidences of money laundering.

Regulation is *'an official rule or the act of controlling something'14*. In this book, it is the act of supervising and controlling operations of MFIs, by the central bank or other official authority. Until the late nineties, the sector was self-regulating, mostly through national associations or networks. Self-regulation was basically voluntary because there were no penalties for those who failed to adhere to standards set by the association or the network. The associations or networks

---

14 *Cambridge Dictionary*

were dominated by the big or the more financially able MFIs, and the small ones did not always feel they had an equal voice. This story of microfinance associations and networks will not be complete without mentioning that these institutions have limped for decades and continue to do so today. Many suffer from inadequate technical capacity and a lack of funding, and the only real value they provide to their members is serving as a conduit for information, limited advocacy and lobbying. In my view, some of the successful microfinance networks include those of Ethiopia and Uganda. The networks have, however, been instrumental in engaging and collaborating with the regulators in the development of new financial inclusion policies, laws and regulations. But they could be more innovative in building capacity of members and improving professional work ethics within the sector.

The new laws and regulations opened opportunities for MFIs to introduce new products and services. As donor funds dwindled, some MFIs ventured into deposit mobilisation, and the central banks were on hand with the respective regulatory framework and ready to fulfil their mandate of protecting public savings. In countries like Kenya, Malawi, Zambia and even Nigeria, regulations governing MFIs have been tailored or customised through stakeholder collaboration in the development of regulations. For example, the minimum capital and capital adequacy are much lower than that of commercial banks. Also, unlike banks, the MFIs are not obligated to follow the Basel reporting framework.

In Uganda, MFIs could not introduce agency banking directly, but they could do so through commercial banks. But in Kenya, the Democratic Republic of Congo (DRC), Nigeria, Zambia and Malawi, the MFIs could introduce agency banking directly. It would seem, that in some markets or rather in most markets, the laws and respective regulations have not been broad enough to allow MFIs to undertake comprehensive banking. MFIs are also not members of the respective clearing houses, and their clearing is still undertaken by commercial banks. Whether they are deposit-taking or not, the MFIs in most countries could not use the word 'bank' or call themselves a bank, but this is different for Nigeria. The central banks also provided guidelines regarding definitions of what would be considered a microloan or micro deposit, which meant that MFIs could not freely move into the SME space. While Kenya has been more liberal with this definition, Nigeria has remained stringent. In Malawi, if the definition was followed, it would stifle the growth of the few MFIs, especially because to be profitable, an MFI requires a mixed portfolio across the MSME spectrum. The banks would be happy to see these definitions implemented while they themselves freely explore the MFI micro space directly or indirectly. The hope is that some regulators, especially those in Southern Africa, can be encouraged to debate and review definitions compared to their compatriots in East and West Africa.

The other significant change that came with the regulation of MFIs is the increased costs, especially those related to compliance. Under the new regulations, the MFIs had to upgrade their infrastructure, especially the banking halls in line with that of banks. They also had to introduce a risk department and realign the board subcommittees. The recruitment of management board and board members had to be approved by the respective central banks, unlike before when the institutions could hire anyone for the top positions and recruit anyone to the board. In this specific aspect, regulation has promoted professionalism within MFIs and enhanced the quality of governance.

These regulatory changes, even though positive, were not without challenges. Not all regulators had the capacity to regulate the sector, given that the central banks are traditionally staffed with bank professionals who might not have interfaced with microfinance or financial inclusion. But the learning within the central banks has been impressive. While some opened up and hired non-bank professionals from the microfinance sector, the majority built their capacity from within. The central banks have gone from uninterested parties to champions or key players within the financial inclusion space. Outside their traditional work, several central banks are now involved, or have been involved, in the promotion of financial literacy, became conduits for low-cost financing from international funders, or guarantee fund managers to promote financial inclusion for both urban and rural sectors.

The central banks have also collaborated with other regulators to promote the implementation of consumer protection principles. Without fear of contradiction, I can assert that microfinance paradigm shifts have helped demystify central banks, who were either unapproachable or ambiguous to the public before the microfinance era, and when only trained economists understood what these banks were about. The central banks opening up and becoming active partners in financial inclusion has encouraged banks to see the good in the microfinance space and encouraged them not to hold tightly to banking as a monopoly or a preserve of the 'haves' but an all-inclusive service where more people now understand banking in a broader sense. There has been more collaboration between players within the overall financial sector, which is a good development for individual countries and the continent in general.

CHAPTER 7

TECHNICAL ADVISORY SERVICES: THE HIGH MAINTAINANCE KID ON THE BLOCK

The story of microfinance will not be complete without touching on the issue of technical advisory services. Technical advisory services within the microfinance industry reminds me of the story of the shipowner repair engineer. The engineer was called, and when he arrived, he inspected the ship from top to bottom, took out a small hammer and hit something gently, and the engine came back to life. Afterwards, the engineer billed the ship owner $20,000, and when the ship owner complained that the bill was too high for the little work or effort the engineer did, the engineer explained that actually $2 was for effort, while the $19,998 was for knowing where to knock![15]

I wish I could say that many of the microfinance technical advisors and consultants were or are like this

---

[15] with *Gokhan Kilinc*. *'Trust Me, I'm an "Engineer"'*

engineer! But I'm afraid I cannot. Many act, or pretend to be, like this engineer, but often, they are not sure what to hit for the engine to come back to life, and often many practise trial and error or hit and miss. I was once an observer in a sales and marketing training session, and one mantra taught to the bank staff by the consultant was, 'Fake it until you make it'[16]! The staff were excited, but I felt sad because I don't believe anyone should be faking anything with other people's lives. The effort used to fake could be more appropriately applied to learning and developing solutions. This approach may obviously have worked for many, but it will not work for everyone! What will work for most people is the experience of knowing where to tap or what to hit.

Technical advisors and consultants come in all shapes and sizes, some very theoretical, some very confident and well-read, while some are simple and practical. But the latter are few. For the many years I have been in the consulting and advisory field, and most times, the rule or precedence is, 'who you know' over 'what you know'. If the technical advisor is a company, their success rate in getting jobs will probably be how big or small the

---

[16] *Famous quote by a social psychologist, Amy Cuddy*

name or brand is, even where a tendering process is followed. But, like them or not, advisors and consultants have been the most versatile through the shifts. They have been able to embrace change quickly and remain relevant within the shifts through self-learning and exposure. They keep themselves up to date with sectorial happenings, and some get involved in research to discover what is working well and where.

Many consultants stay connected and learn from one another. But our friends from the west do better at networking and introducing one another and sharing opportunities. As Africans, we are sometimes a little selfish, and we rarely share opportunities with each other, sometimes getting ourselves involved in some unhealthy competition and maybe even a little jealousy along the way. Some African brothers and sisters would rather let an opportunity pass by as opposed to having someone they know get it. I guess it is the way the Almighty created us! Maybe I should not be dragging God into that situation, for we all have the mind and freedom to make choices. Twice and in different countries and times, I got invited to bid for consulting jobs, and because I could not do it alone, I contacted two colleagues, respectively, so we could team up and submit the bid together. Coincidently they both went behind my back and submitted their own bids with prices much lower than I would normally charge. Each got the respective assignment, and we parted ways with one, but one has remained a colleague at a distance to date. I also remember and occasionally tell of one sad story where another close friend and colleague got hired by some international funding agency. I hoped that she would introduce me or at least share the opportunities, but she never did, and I never understood why. But a few years down the line, I got introduced to the same institution by a friend from the west, and I also came across opportunities, which I made sure to introduce others to. Only then did I understand that introducing or referring someone for a job requires one to trust the abilities or capacity of the person, otherwise, the referrer's reputation could be at risk. I understood then why my African sister did not introduce or share the opportunities she came across: she probably did not have confidence I would execute the assignment as per expectation. For that is my own guideline, I will only introduce or refer someone if I'm absolutely certain they will execute the assignment properly. My African sister is forgiven, and we are still friends.

The advisors and consultants are paid to identify problems and propose solutions or other times to articulate the challenges and respective solutions. But some have not identified but only documented challenges and solutions as suggested by the practitioners. Other times, their recommendations are good, but not practical and hence remain in the reports. One weakness I have come across is in regard to general development consultants who cut across sectors and are neither specialists nor subject matter experts. Their advice and recommendations are more usable at the management level but not at field or client level.

Compared to the practitioners, consultants are paid well, and I guess such high pay compensates for not only their knowledge and skill, but intermittency of work. However, there has always been a big disparity between international consultants' pay and that of local consultants. I once worked for a project that paid international advisors/consultants up to $1500 per day while paying local consultants $350 per day, yet they come with similar qualifications and experience. The local consultants sometimes even have a better experience because of the context. But I guess to explain the disparities we must ask the question, whose money is it?

A few years back, I received an invitation to be part of a team to undertake a second design of a rural finance project. I inquired what had happened to the first design team, and I was informed, albeit informally, that they had gone to the country as experts, or 'know it alls' as one government official put it. When the government representatives critiqued the proposed design and asked them questions on specific aspects of the design, they became defensive and rubbed the government officials up the wrong way, and the government in that country refused to have anything further to do with that design team. This did not jeopardise only that specific design, but the overall partnership with the government in relation to other existing projects. The second group, mostly regional and local consultants, were hired to do damage control, which they did successfully. They understood not only the government system, but the cultural context, and this resulted in a successful project over a seven-year period.

The local consultants are told, 'Take it or leave it' while the international consultants may negotiate. I'm not sure why the funders or donors find it easier to pay the international consultants $1500 a day than give this amount to the MFIs for operational expenses. Where big companies bid and win as technical advisors or consultants, they would usually hire local consultants at the same rate of $350 while billing the donors over $1000. So, the MF or financial inclusion sector is the money-making industry for some consulting and advisory firms. If these consultants were making money and the sector was thriving in parallel based on their inputs, then perhaps there would be no need for much debate, but the disconnect and sometimes the quality of some of the work leaves a lot to be desired. While the quality of processes, reports and training can be evaluated instantly, the proposed solutions in terms of institutional building are difficult to evaluate, especially since the consultants are not there to implement or guide the implementation.

From my experience, the best consultants are the ones with an operational background. They have been operators at one time in their careers, and they find it easy to identify strengths and weaknesses with the institution. Their solutions, capacity building, training and mentoring are practice-based, and they don't stop at what needs to be done but also recommend how to implement it. But this consultant is not common. In one project I was supervising in one country, I was helping the project team review the terms of reference for a planned consulting assignment, and one requirement that caught my attention was that the candidates should have knowledge and experience in both rural finance and digital finance. I advised the programme staff to review the requirements if they needed to identify the right person/s, and they asked me why. My answer was simple: 'It is difficult to talk about rural finance and digital finance in one sentence.' The ideal approach at the time was to look for two consultants. Even though this situation has slowly changed, I was not too surprised recently when I joined a team to undertake a country evaluation, and the country project team explained that one reason project implementation has been slower, or sometimes the expected results were not achieved, was because getting experts with the exact fit with requirements was and is still difficult, so they were forced to select candidates who showed strengths in some areas. What would happen then is that the experts would concentrate and overachieve in their area of strength while the other focus areas would remain unsatisfactory or underdeveloped.

To help or ensure technical services and consultancies add value to the institutions, there is a need to develop detailed terms of reference with specific targets and guidelines. Where these are abstract or ambiguous, the consultants or advisors may not be blamed for doing a shoddy job. Experience is important, but having team leaders who are good mentors is also important. A mix of both international and national consultants is vital to align the most up-to-date innovations, practices and local contexts. Effective technical services require not only abstract thinking but good abilities in listening, probing and writing. The latter is because most assignments end up with a report, and the reports should be easy to read and understand, articulating the background, progress and the way of the future.

Training MFI Bank staff (Uganda 2019)

CONCLUSION

The microfinance journey in Africa has been quite a detour with exciting moments and great results, especially the increase of those accessing financial services and the prominence of microfinance and subsequently financial inclusion over the years. The sector has emerged and evolved as part of each country's economy, albeit with mixed results. Microfinance, in its various forms, has diluted elite banking and made it a service accessible and usable by everybody. Microfinance has made banking more friendly.

While I believe it has contributed to better livelihoods and survival, its contribution to MSME growth is still debatable to others. For those in the sector, the debate is not about growth contribution but materiality, and again this is different for every country. The sector players are happy with the progress made. If there was no progress, why would governments pay attention or get involved through policies and laws? Why would non-traditional and commercial players be interested? As children of microfinance, many of us have crawled, walked and ran with the sector. We have understood that we don't work for the client but with the client. We have also understood that microfinance is not a favour, but a service, and nothing is constant. Technology has proved there is no limit to adaptation, and such adaptation is not discriminatory, it does not divide between rural and urban, poor and rich.

Although the sector is not perfect, it stands one on one with other sectors. But which industry or sector is perfect? There are things that can be done better, and these include customer centricity, which needs to espouse the protection of the consumer on a par with the protection of the provider. A little more transparency and professionalism will not hurt but will improve the sector. The distance covered is probably a minute fraction of the distance remaining to be covered. The institutions need to run their show for themselves and their clients, not for funders, donors or governments. Africa and Africans have the capacity to run their show, but they need to learn to tell their own stories in their own words. They need to love themselves, each other and their work more.

The sector players need to accept that change is now constant and develop the need to always look for ways to change and evolve. Microfinance is no longer a preserve, and if it is to be done well, the players need to embrace alliances and collaboration with the broader financial sector players. Competition and co-existence are possible, and human capital management is paramount for success. While systems are important, they cannot take precedence over people.

Re-positioning and re-branding are one way to go. Digital is here to stay, and being digitally savvy is no longer an option but a priority not only for the institutions but for their staff.

.

www.ingramcontent.com/pod-product-compliance
Lightning Source LLC
Chambersburg PA
CBHW070359220526
45467CB00001B/437